Month-by-Month
Clip Art

With CD

SCHOLASTIC

NEW YORK • TORONTO • LONDON • AUCKLAND • SYDNEY

MEXICO CITY • NEW DELHI • HONG KONG • BUENOS AIRES

Editor: Maria L. Chang
Cover design by Ka-Yeon Kim-Li
Interior design by Susan Isaacs
Illustrations by Karen Sevaly

ISBN-13: 978-0-545-11924-5
ISBN-10: 0-545-11924-3
Copyright © 2009 by Teacher's Friend, a Scholastic Company
All rights reserved.
Printed in the U.S.A.

5 6 7 8 9 10   40   15 14 13 12 11 10

Table of Contents

Welcome to Month-by-Month Clip Art With CD!

If you're one of those people who spends hours looking for just the right piece of clip art to enhance your classroom newsletter or bulletin board, then this book is for you! In the pages that follow, you'll find hundreds of black-line clip-art designs, each one carefully selected to meet your monthly educational needs. Looking for a Dalmatian wearing a firefighter's hat to remind students of Fire Safety Month in October? Go to page 29. How about a large turkey to help you invite parents to your class's Thanksgiving celebration? See page 38. Need a kid-friendly image of Abraham Lincoln for Presidents Day? Check out page 75.

Use our wide selection of original clip art, organized by month, to welcome students back to school, celebrate holidays and special events, teach about Pilgrims and presidents, create picture cards for learning games, and more. You can use this art to decorate your letters to parents, student handouts, or announcements. You can also create certificates of achievement, bookmarks, or stationery. There are even blank calendar templates that you can fill in to remind students and parents of field trips and other important dates for the month.

Best of all, this book includes a CD that features the same clip art—in color and in black and white—in a ready-to-use .png format that you can drop into your computer documents, presentations, interactive whiteboard, or Web page. Image files are labeled with their corresponding page numbers so you can easily cross-reference them with the clip art in the book.

Throughout the year, you'll find yourself going back to this book and CD again and again for your decorating, graphic, and educational needs. Have fun!

September

Sunday	Monday	Tuesday	Wednesday	Thursday	Friday	Saturday

School Glue

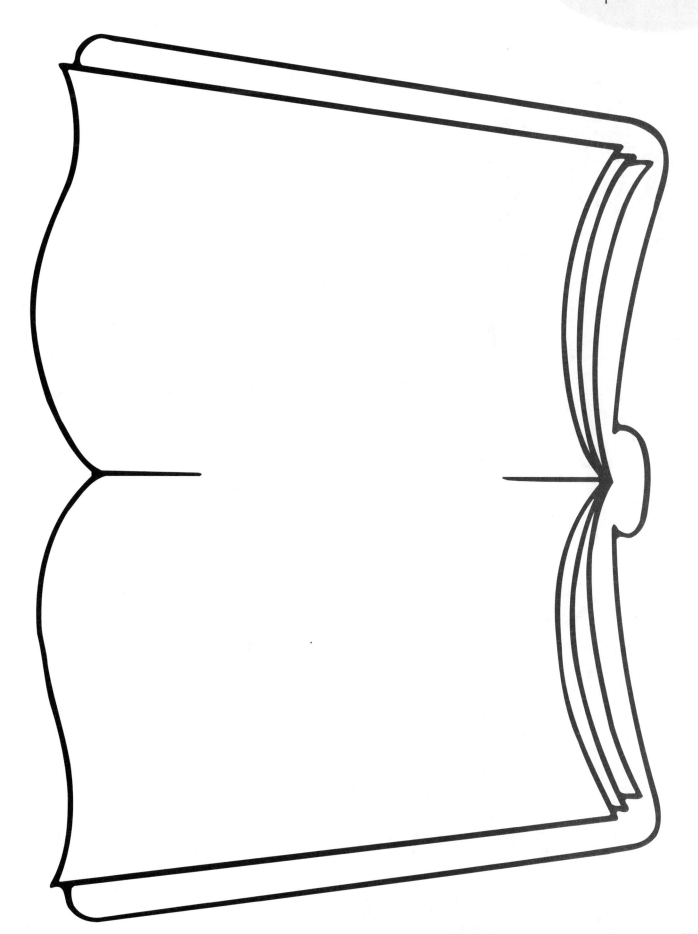

September

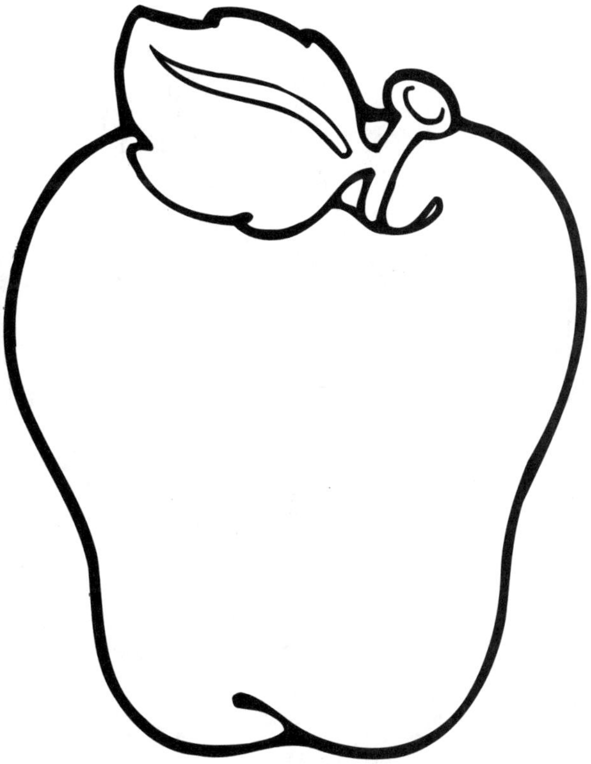

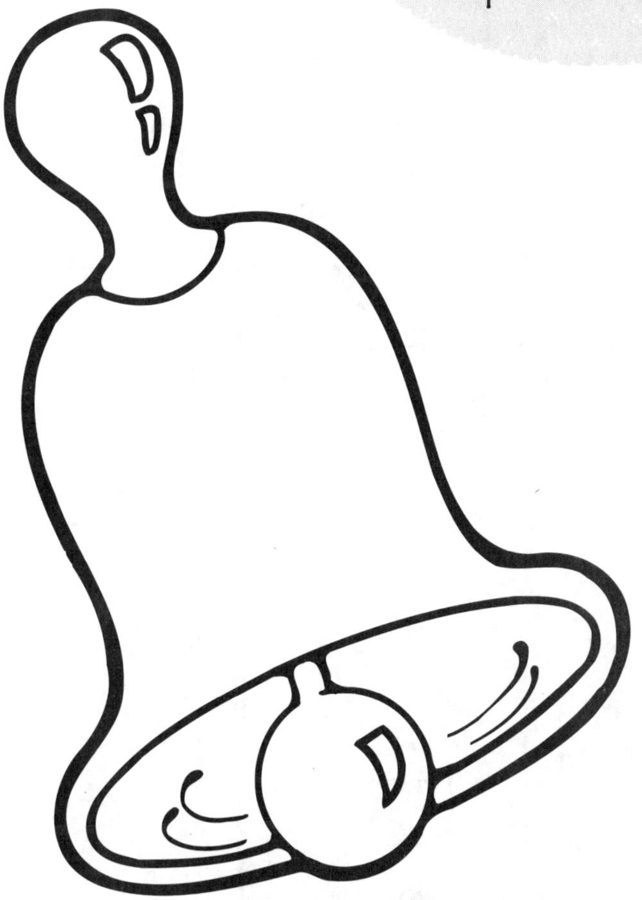

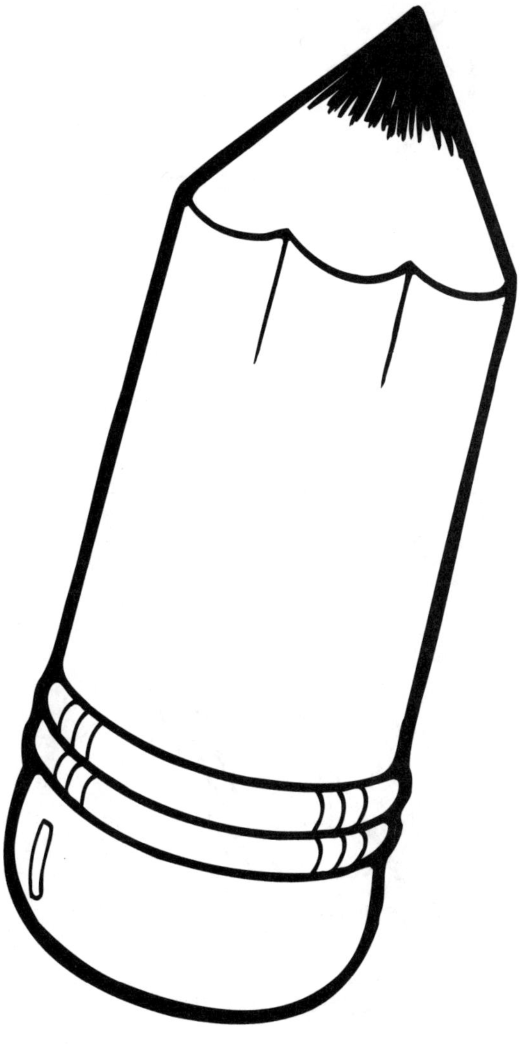

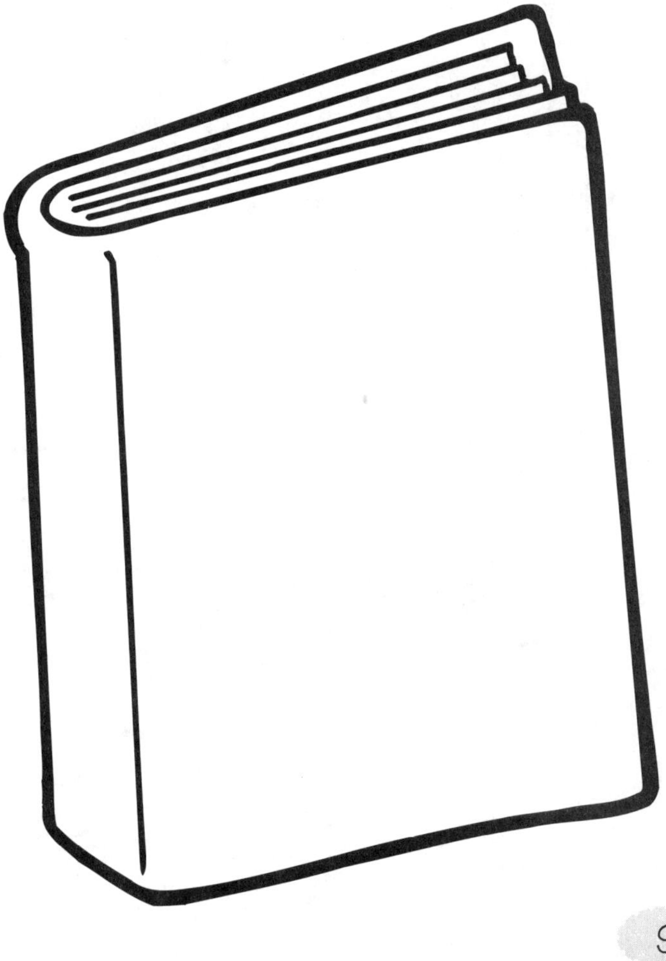

September

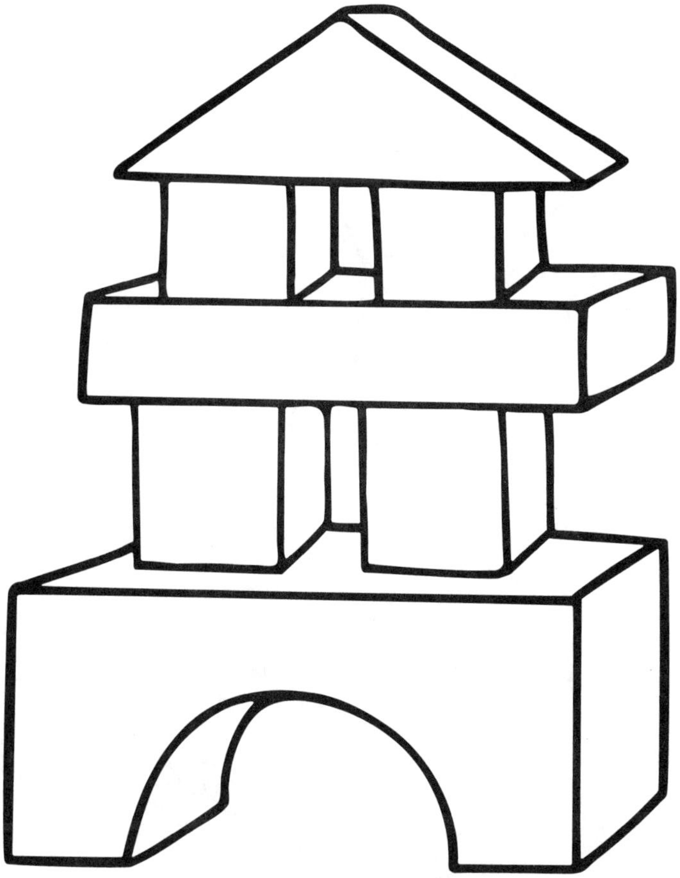

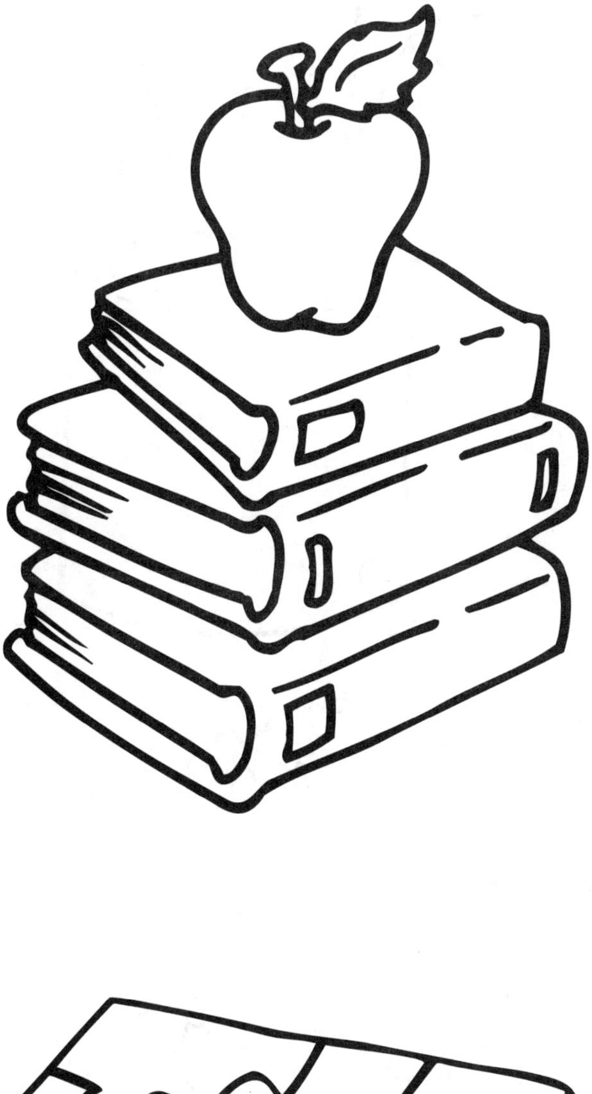

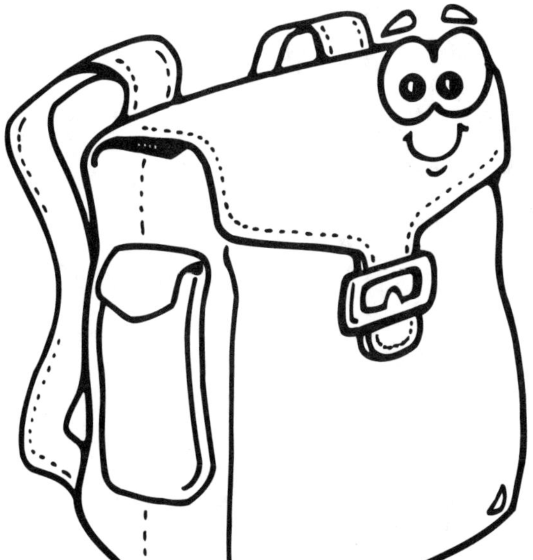

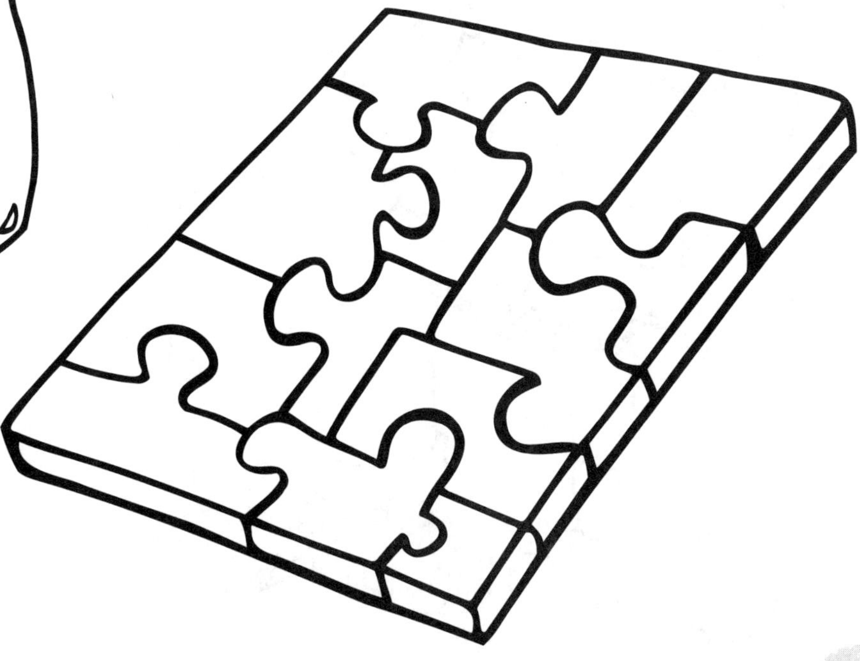

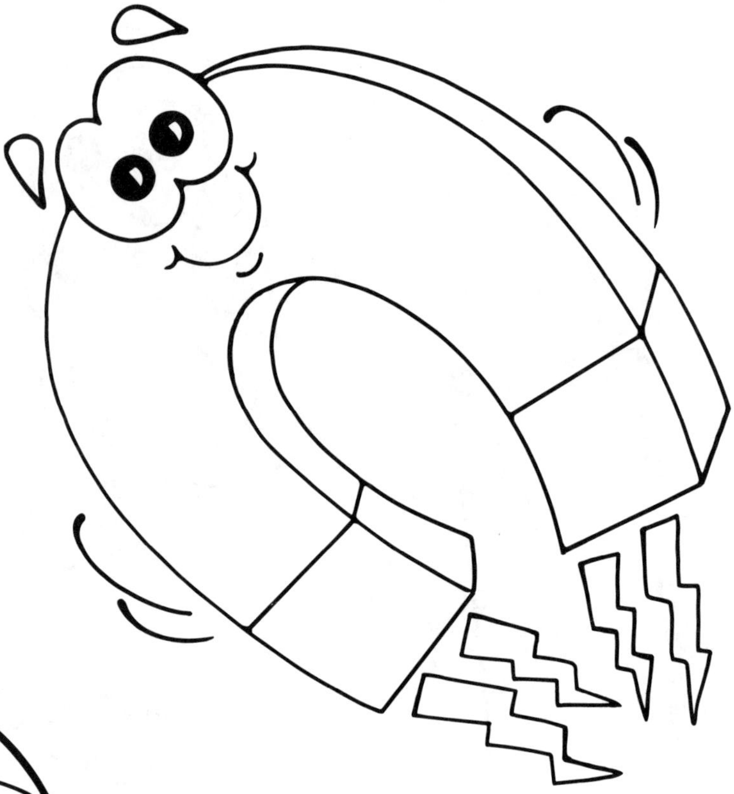

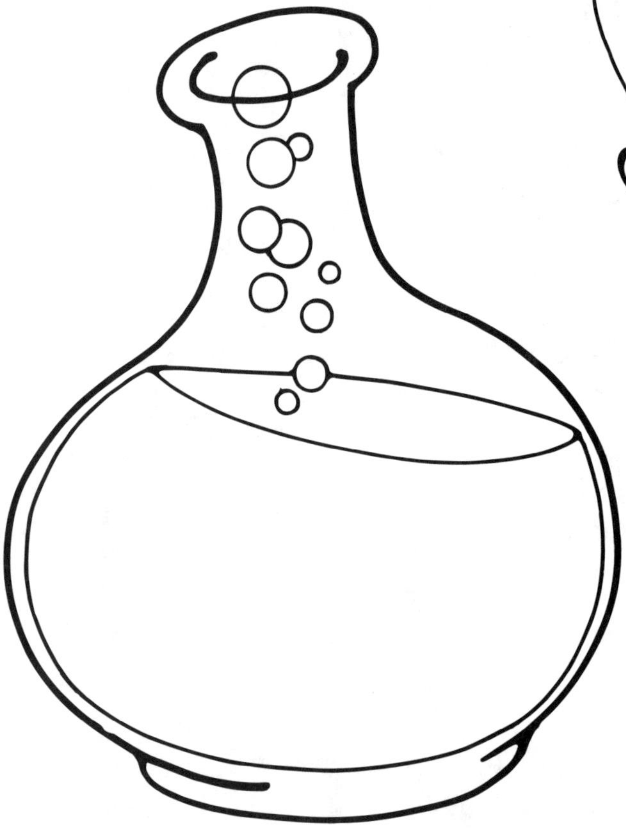

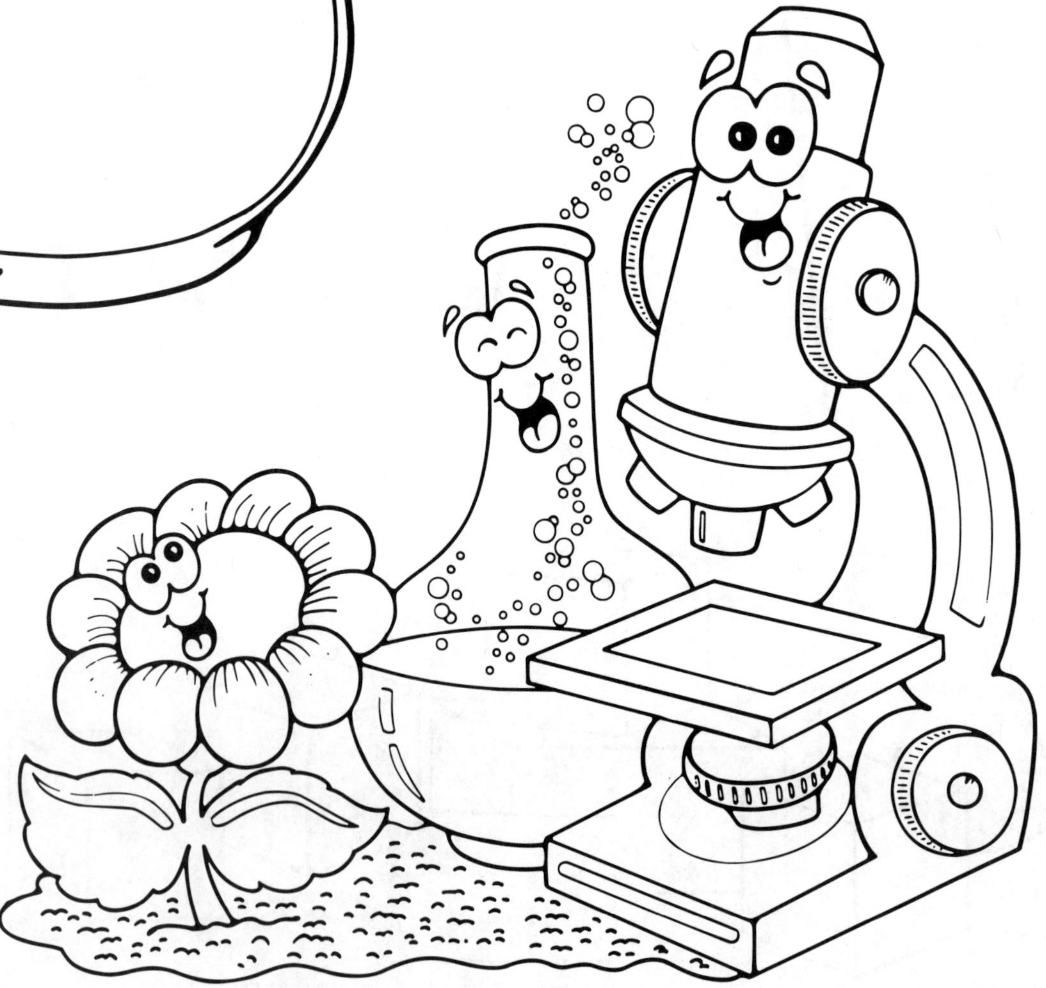

My Name is...

September

October

Sunday	Monday	Tuesday	Wednesday	Thursday	Friday	Saturday

Awesome Autumn!

25

November

Sunday	Monday	Tuesday	Wednesday	Thursday	Friday	Saturday

November

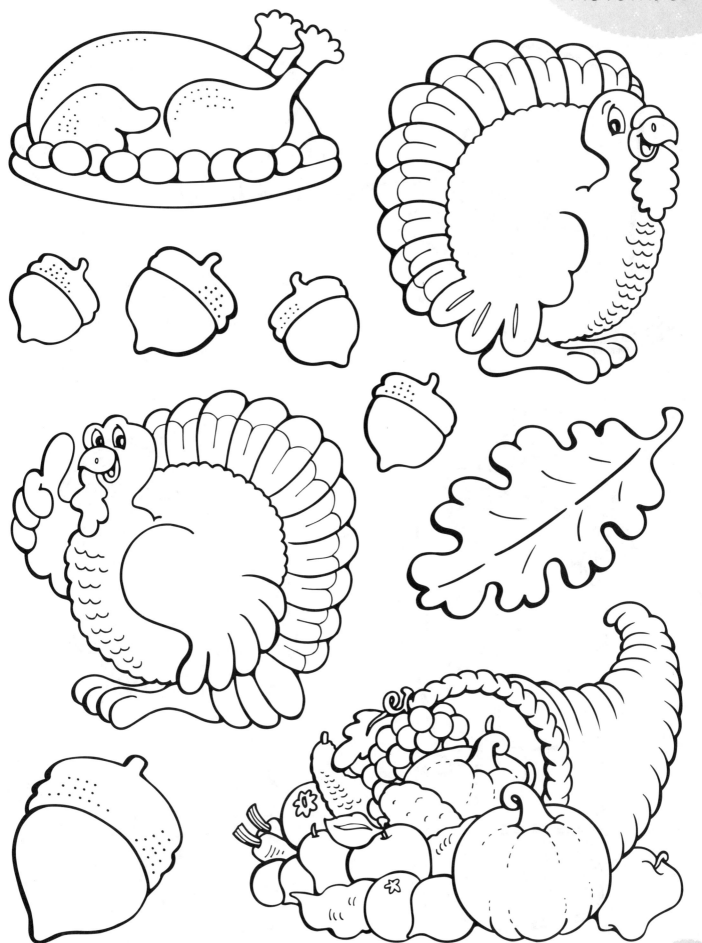

November

34

November

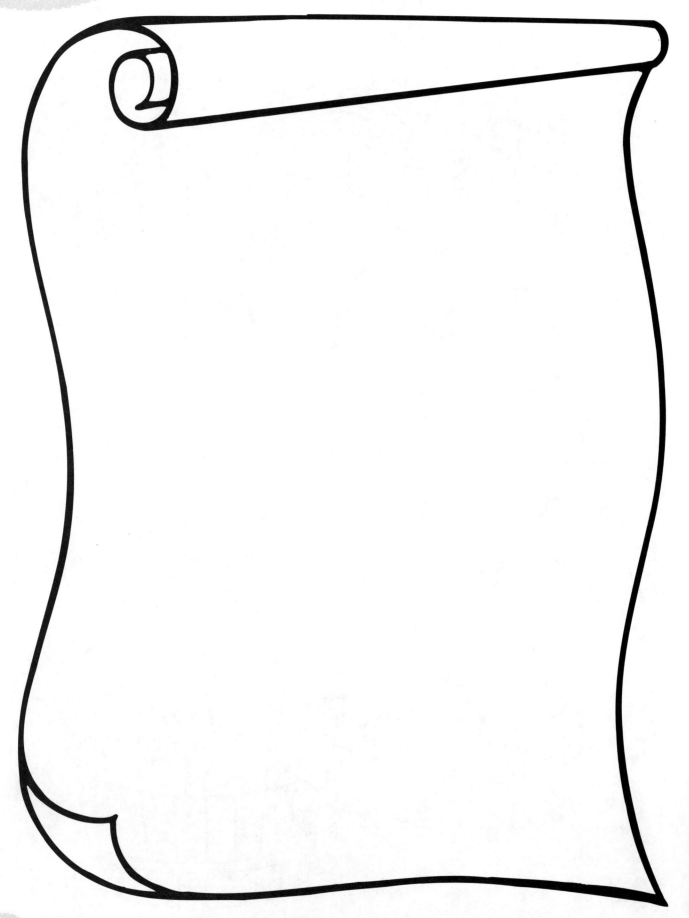

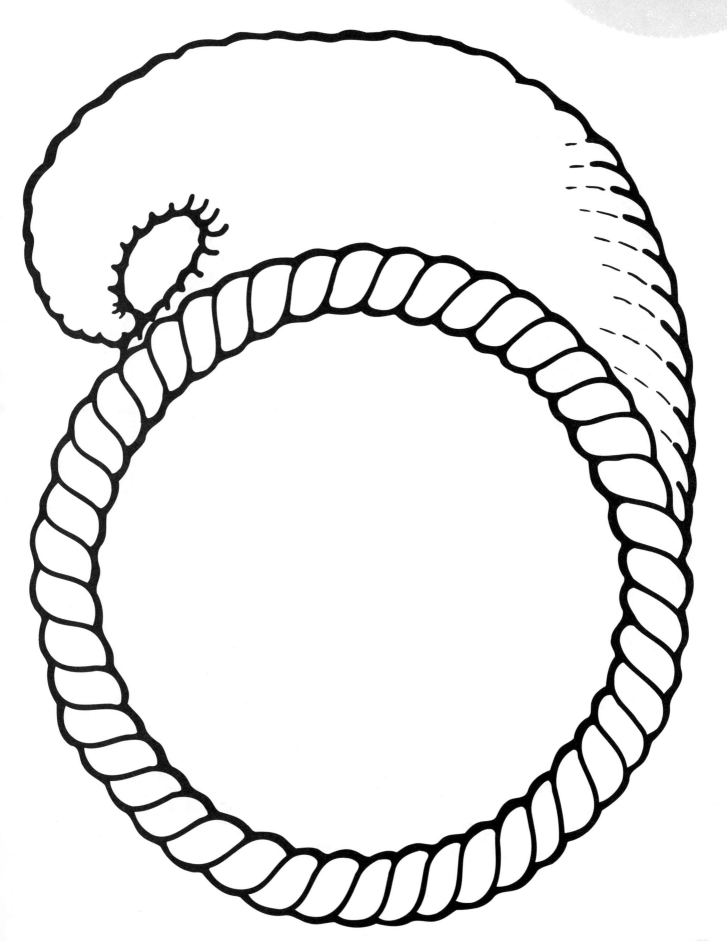

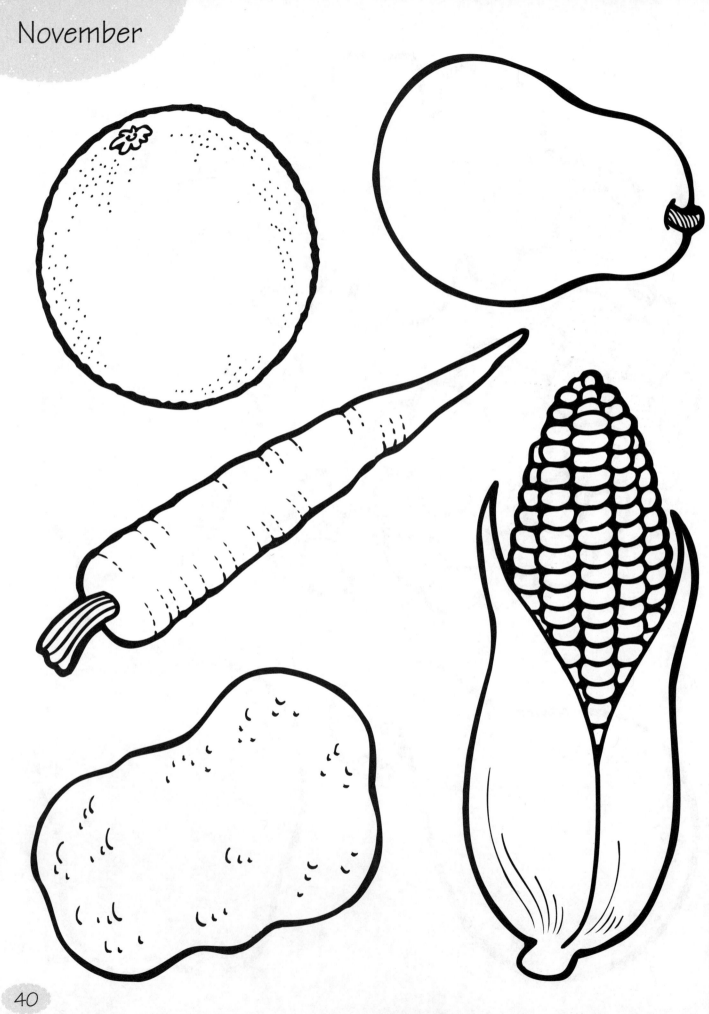

November

42

December

Sunday	Monday	Tuesday	Wednesday	Thursday	Friday	Saturday

43

December

December

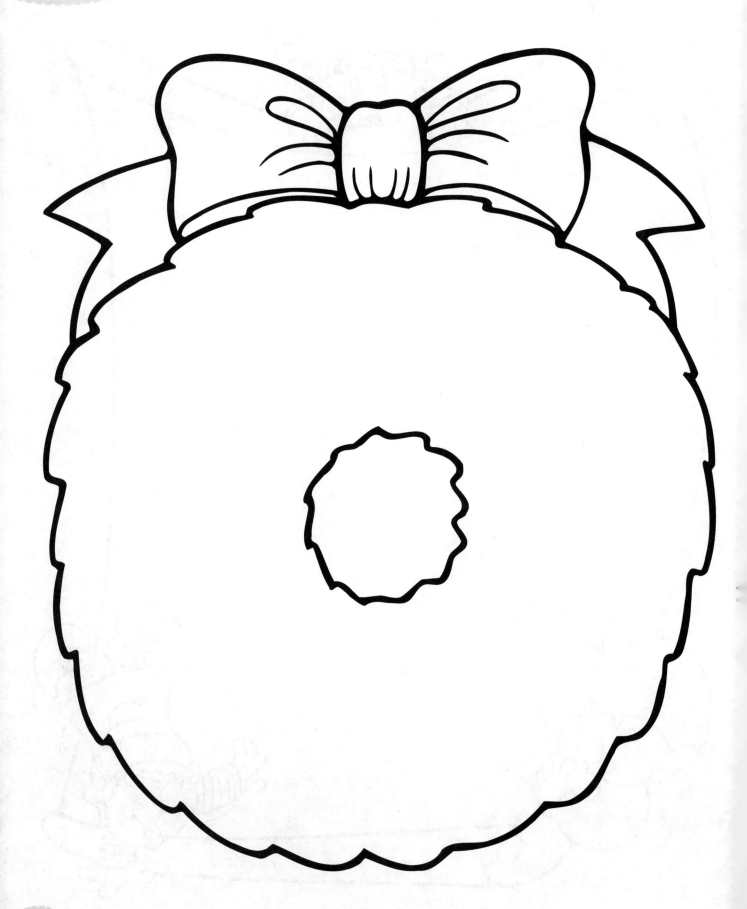

48

December

49

December

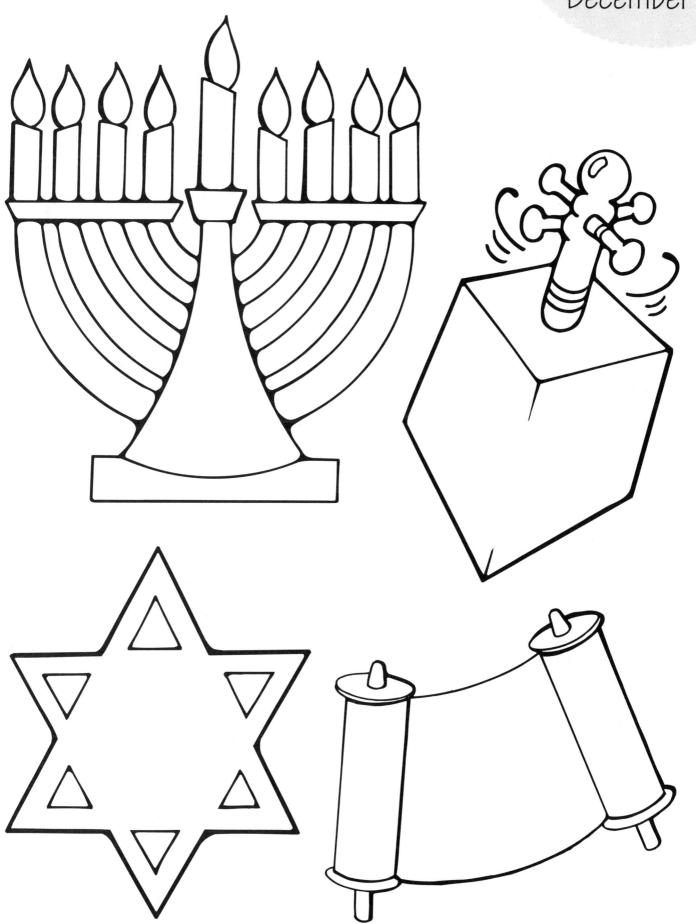

HAPPY KWANZAA

January

Sunday	Monday	Tuesday	Wednesday	Thursday	Friday	Saturday

January

Winter Wonderland!

58

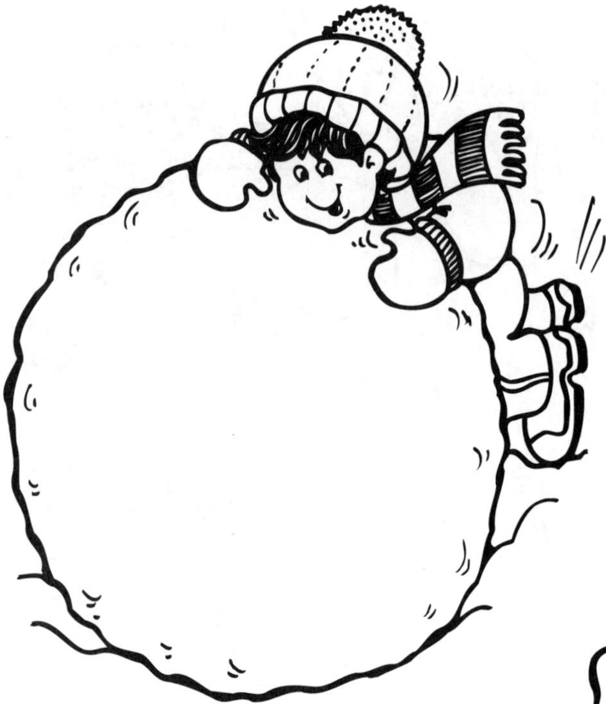

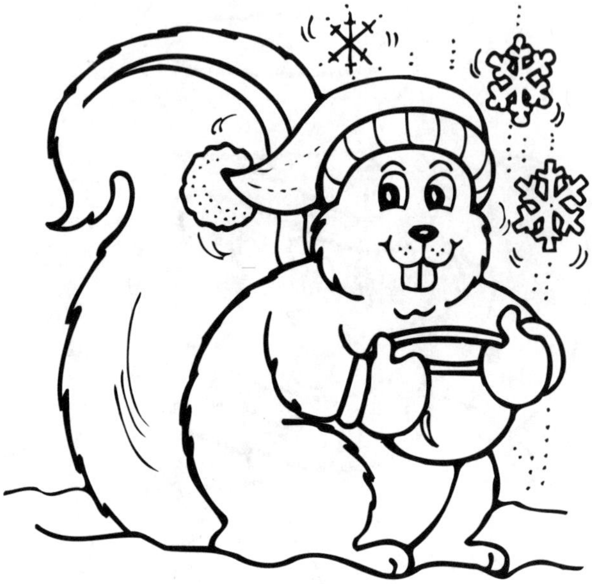

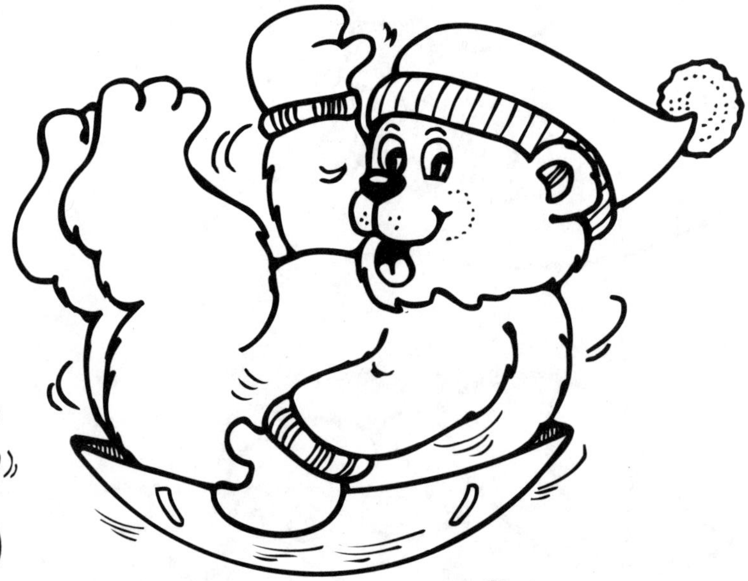

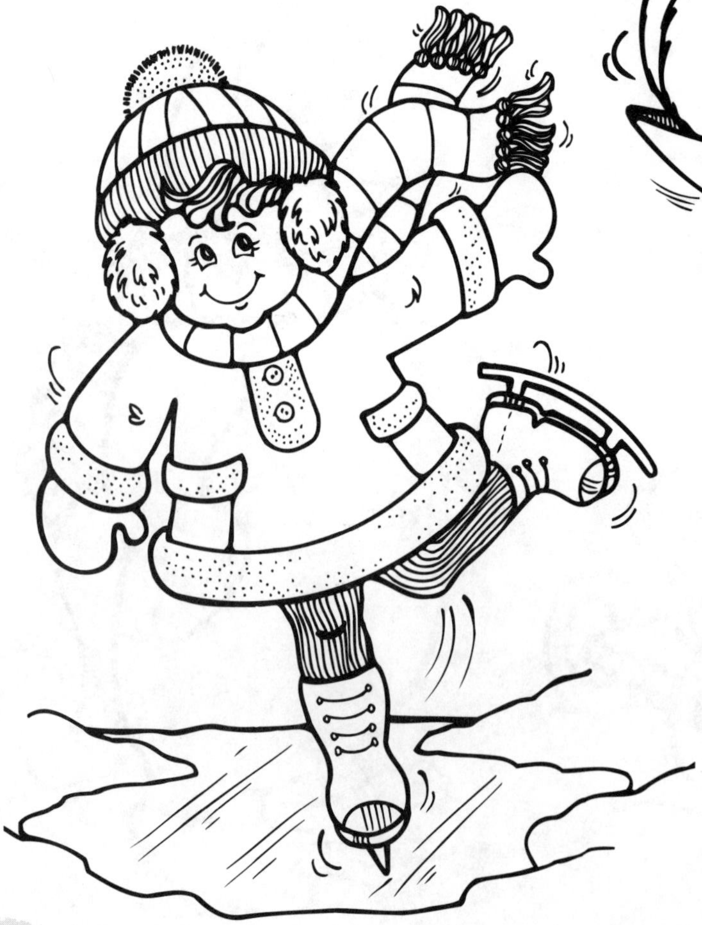

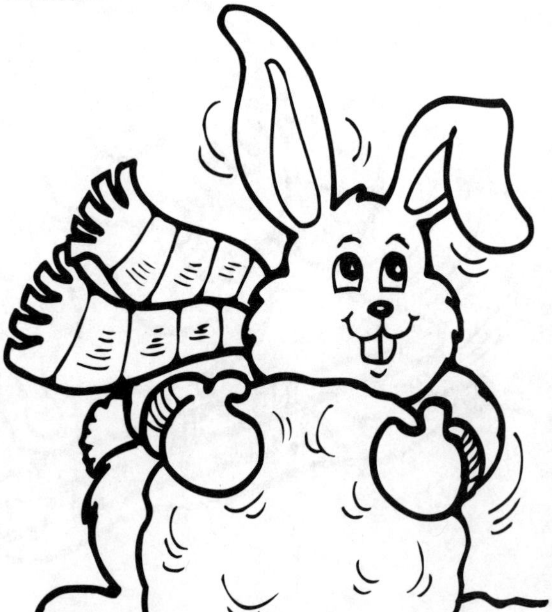

January

February

Sunday	Monday	Tuesday	Wednesday	Thursday	Friday	Saturday

February

February

BE MINE

LUV U

SWEET

69

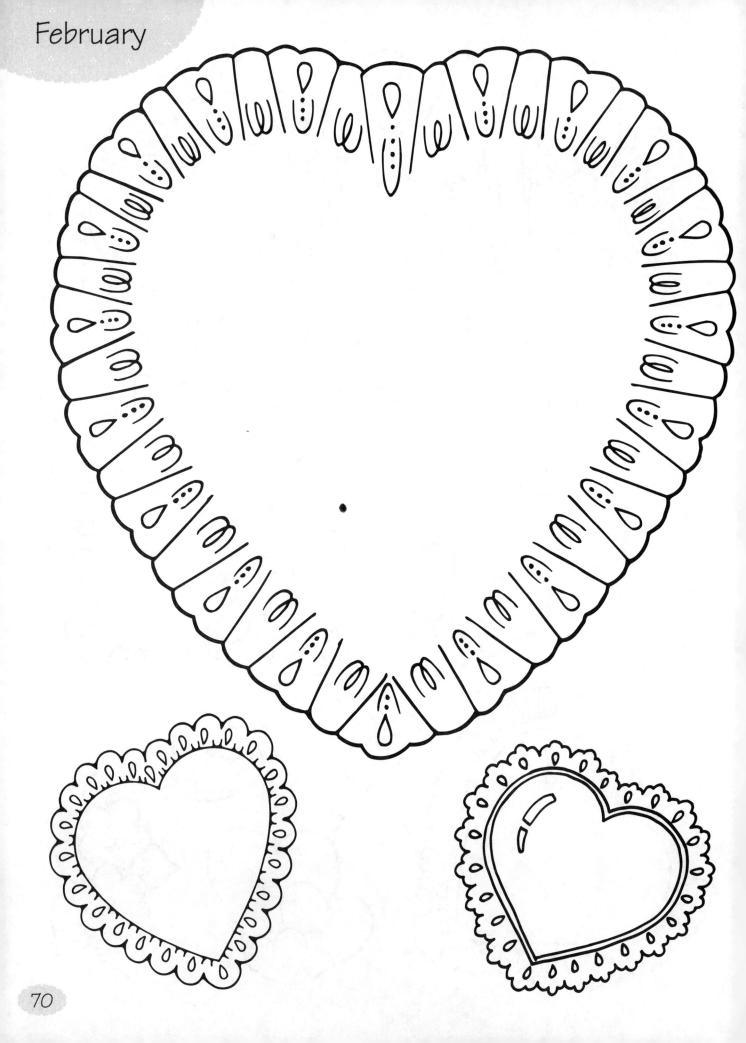

February

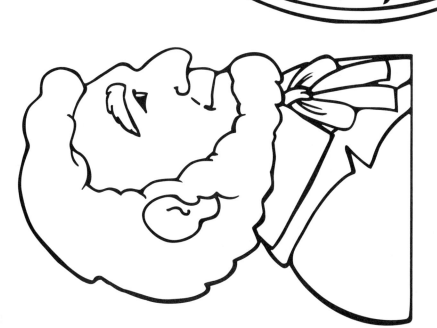

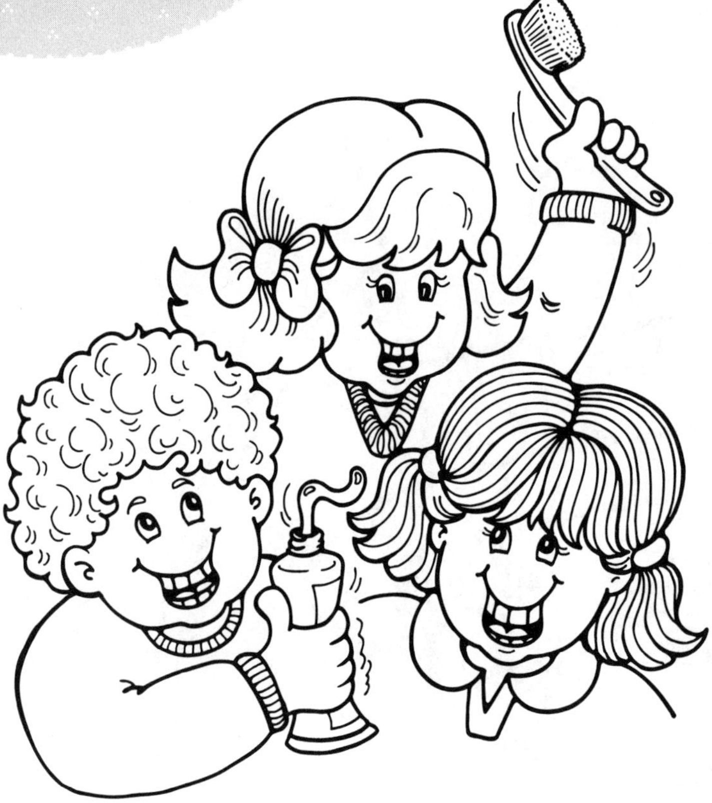

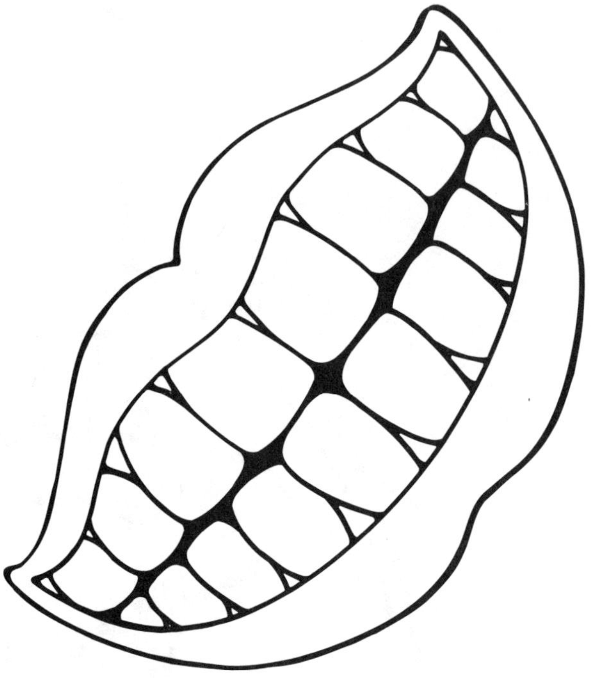

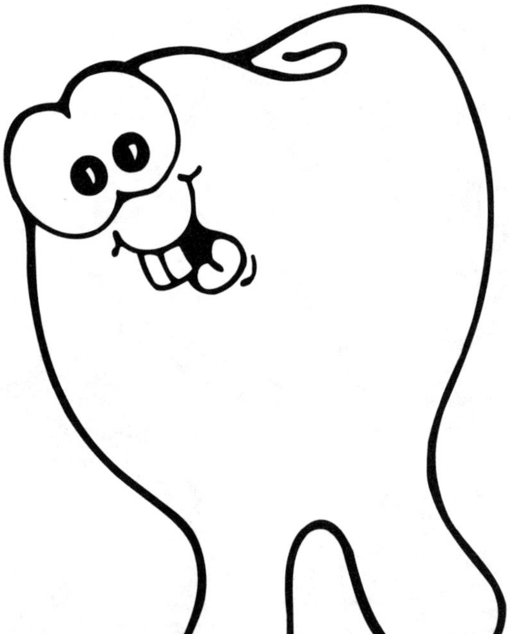

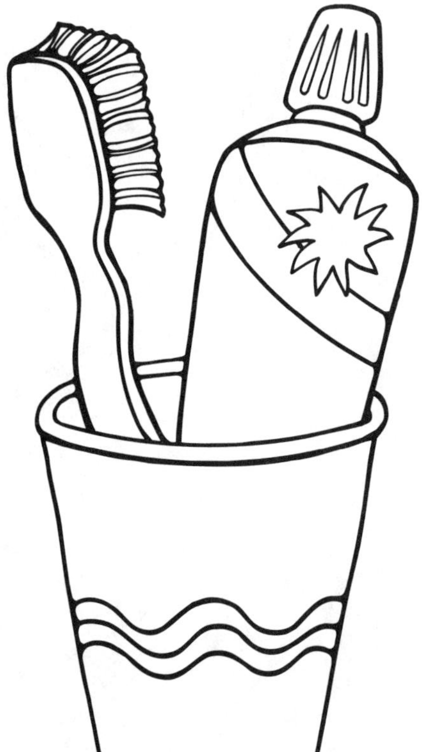

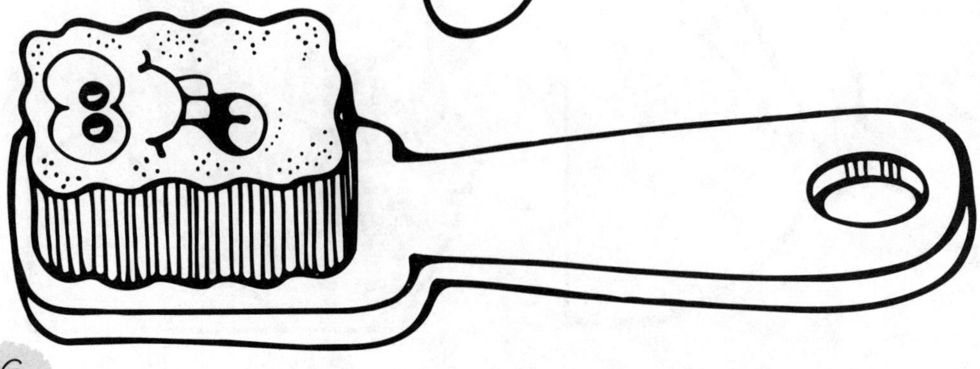

March

Sunday	Monday	Tuesday	Wednesday	Thursday	Friday	Saturday

SOAP

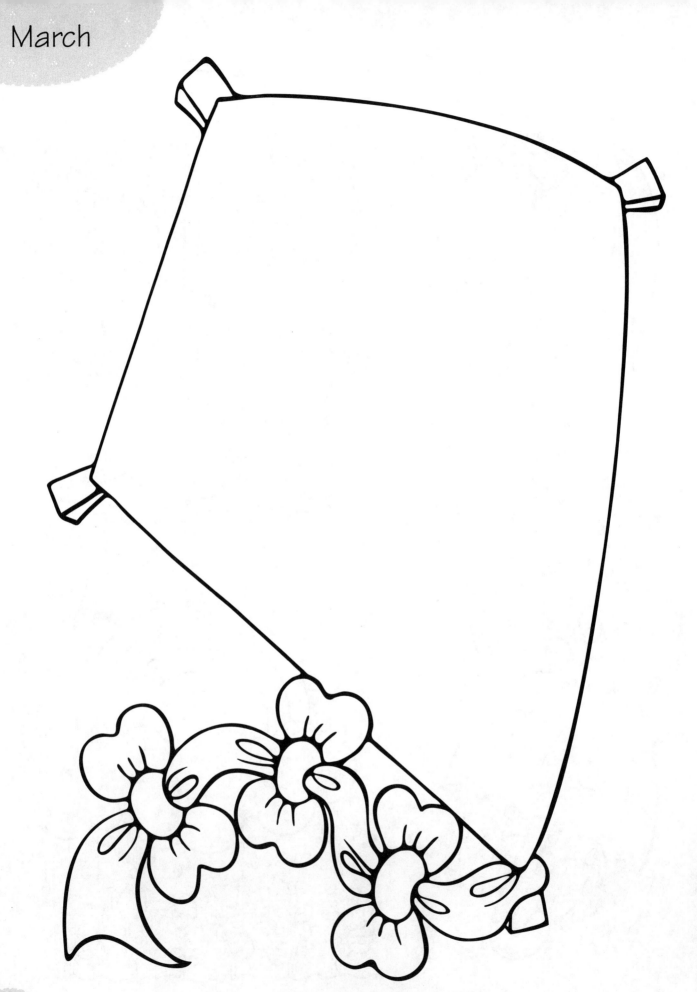

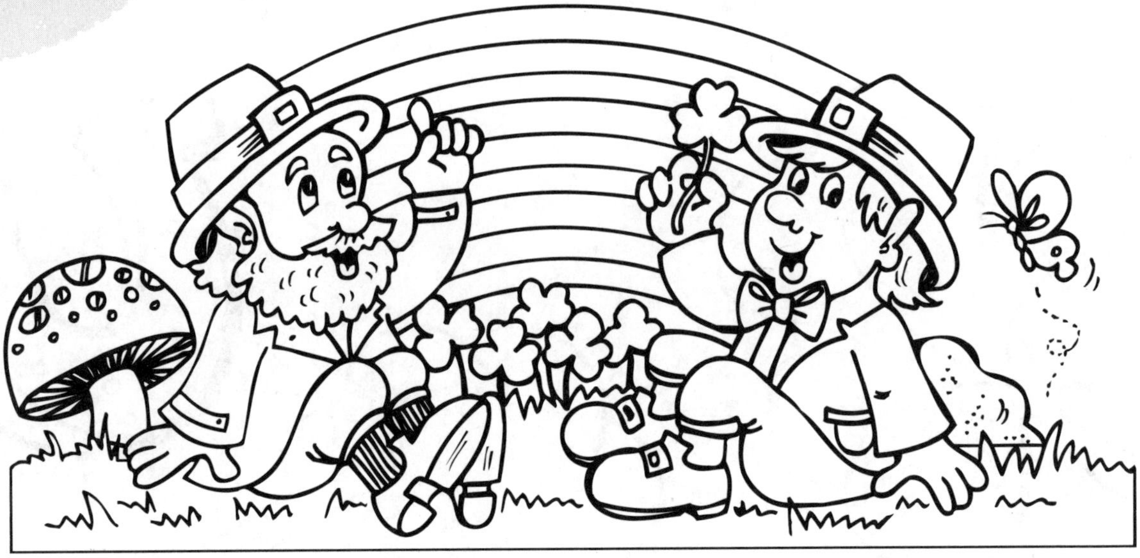

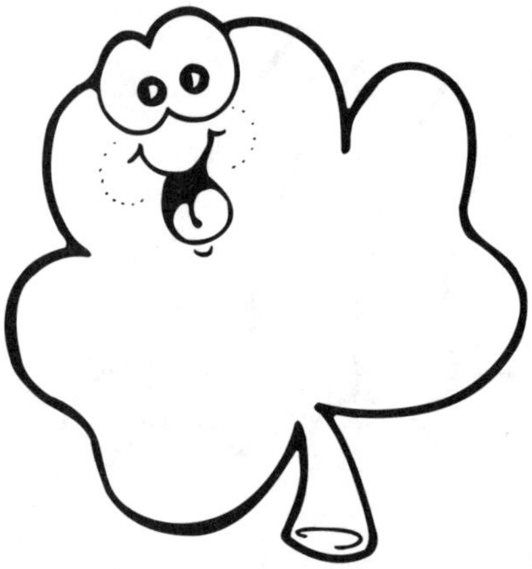

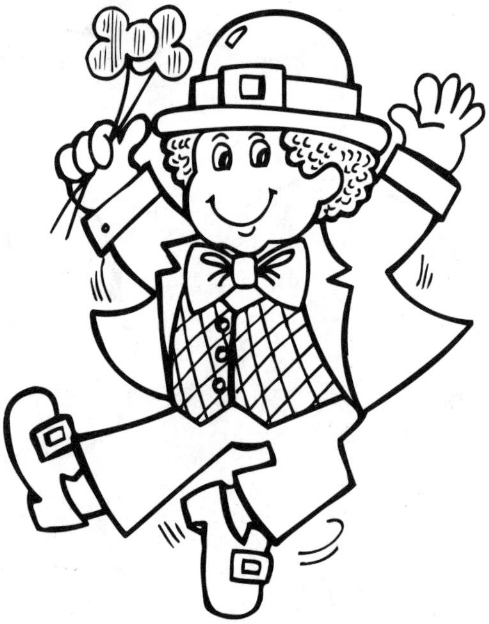

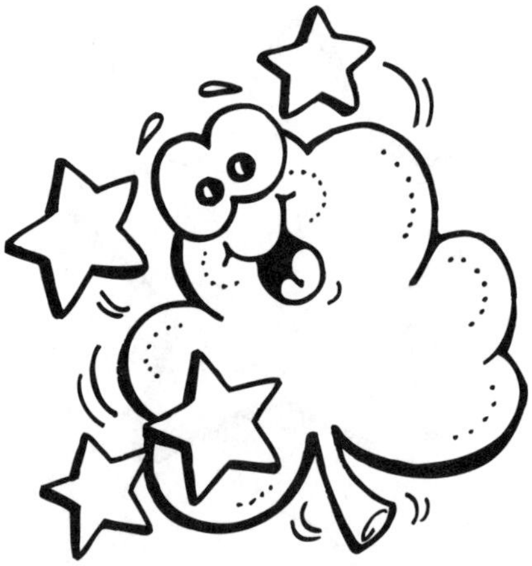

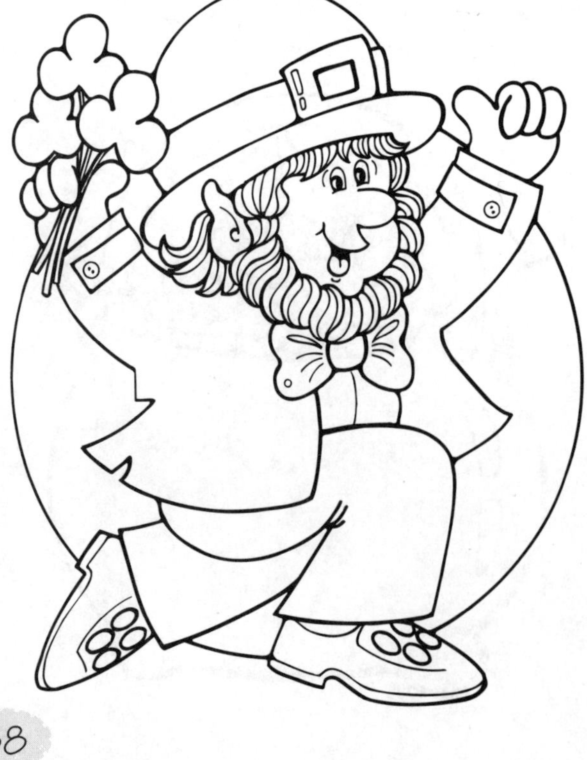

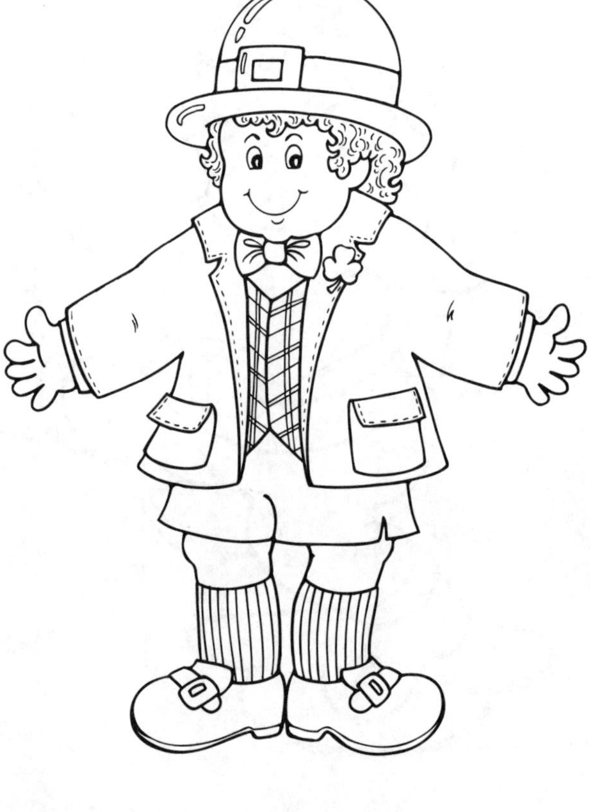

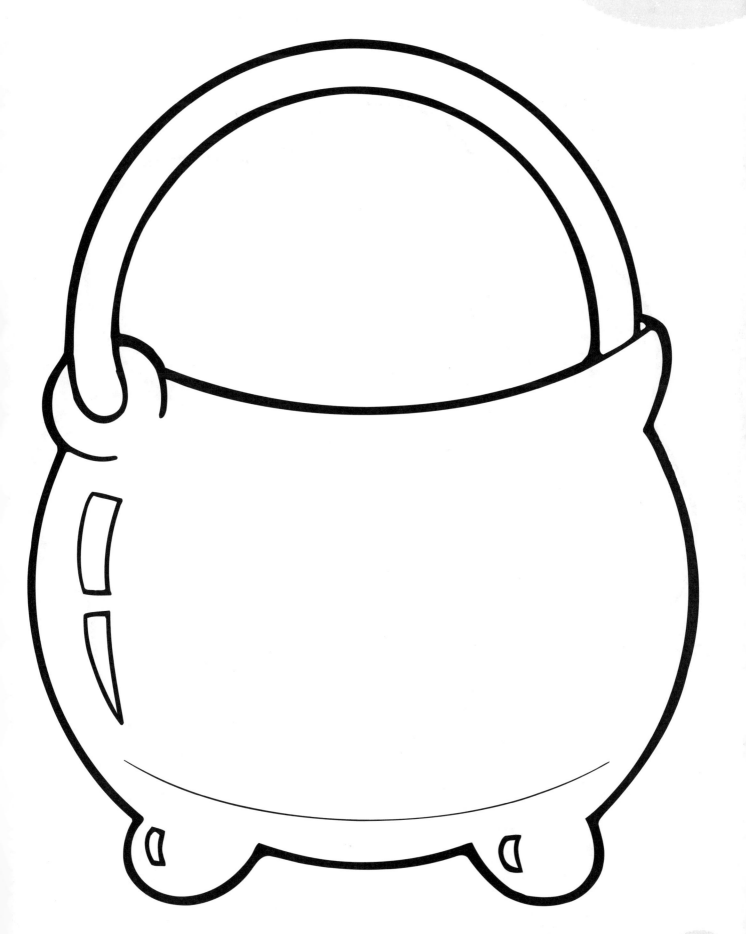

April

Sunday	Monday	Tuesday	Wednesday	Thursday	Friday	Saturday

Happy Easter!

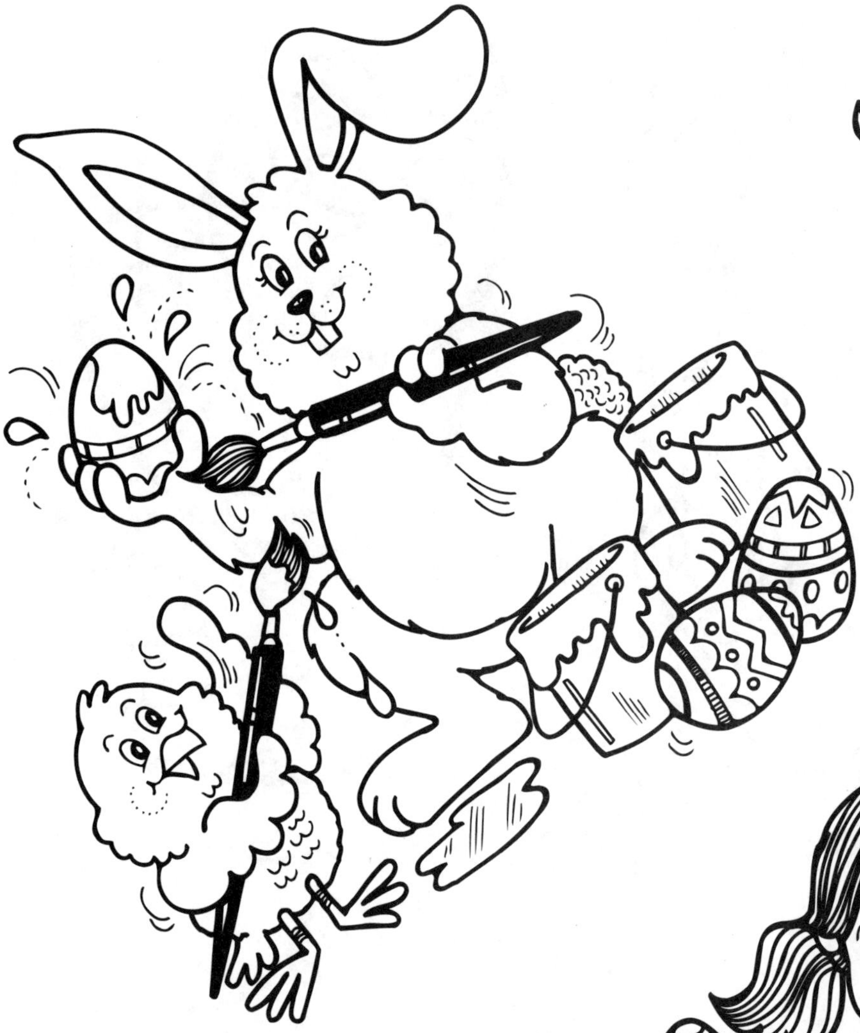

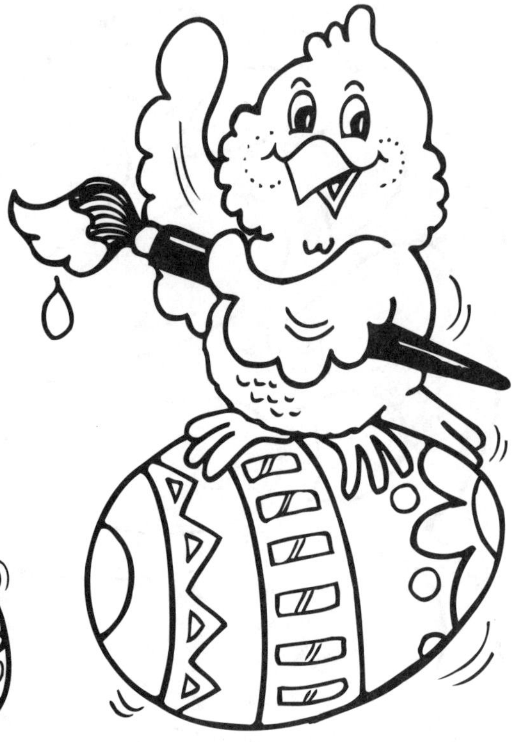

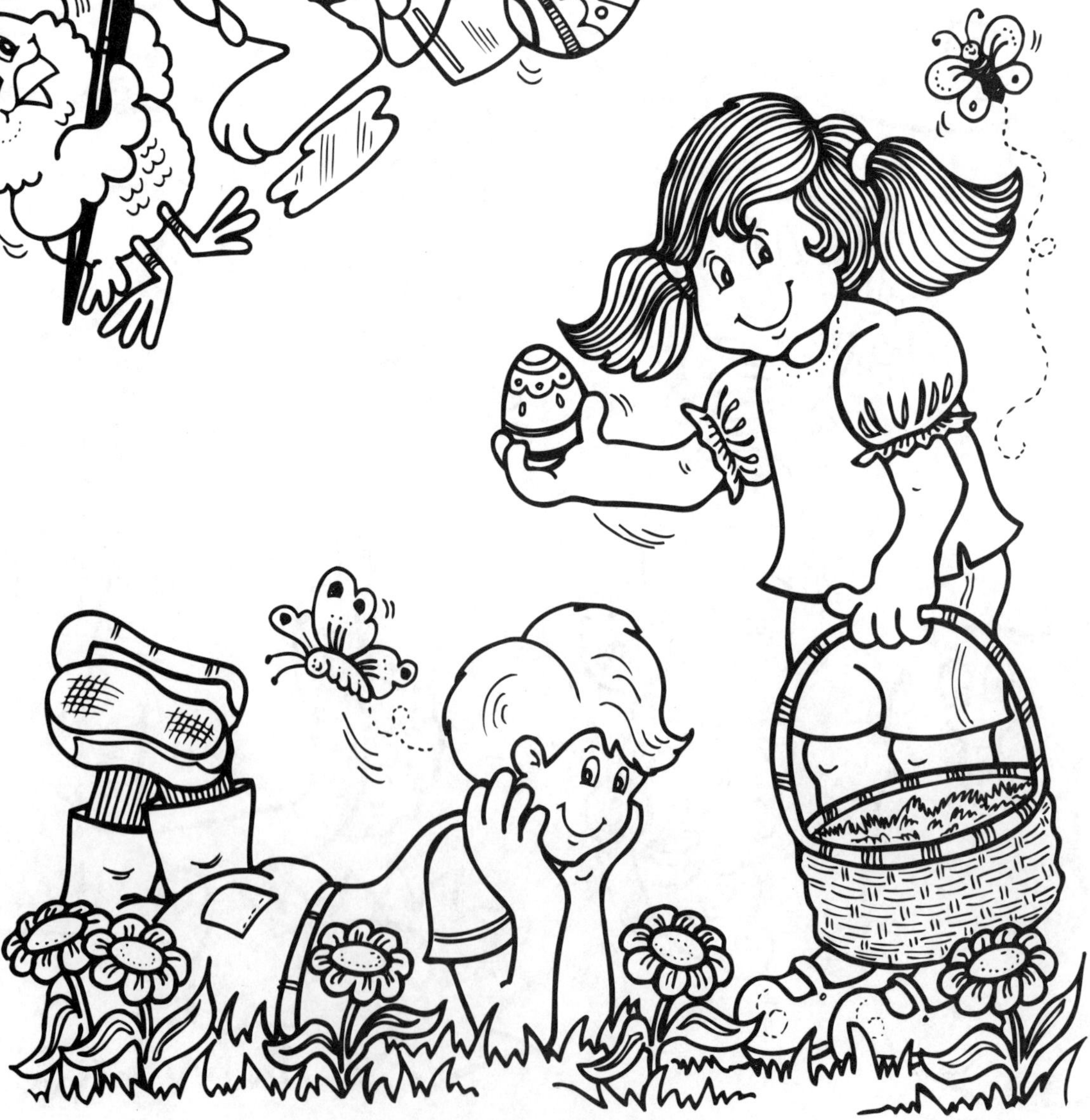

April

95

April

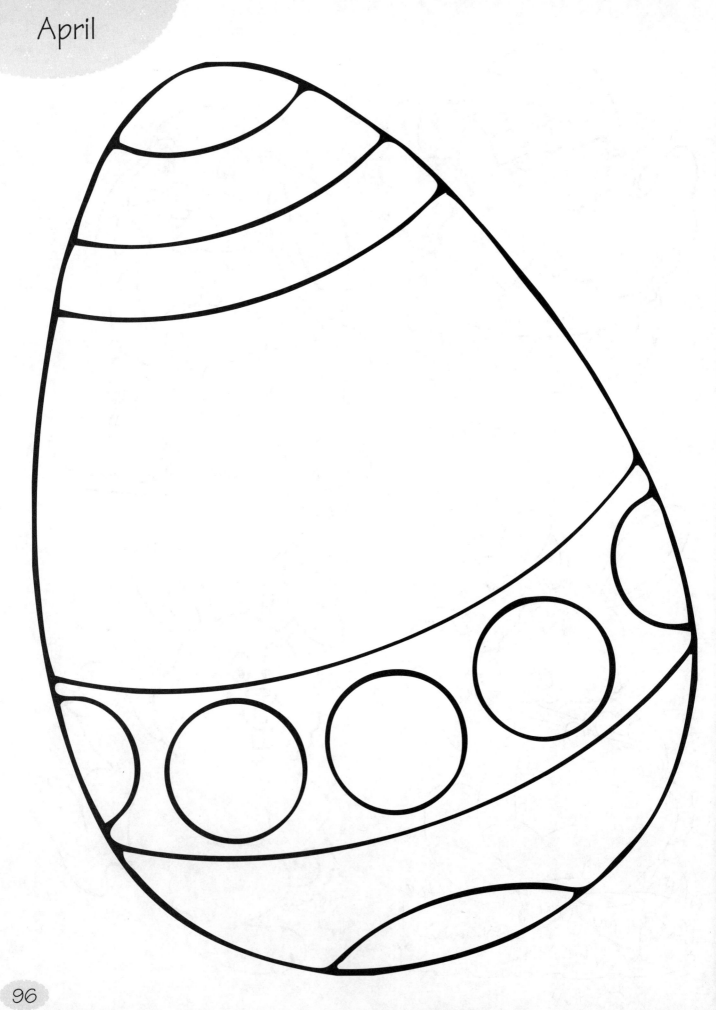

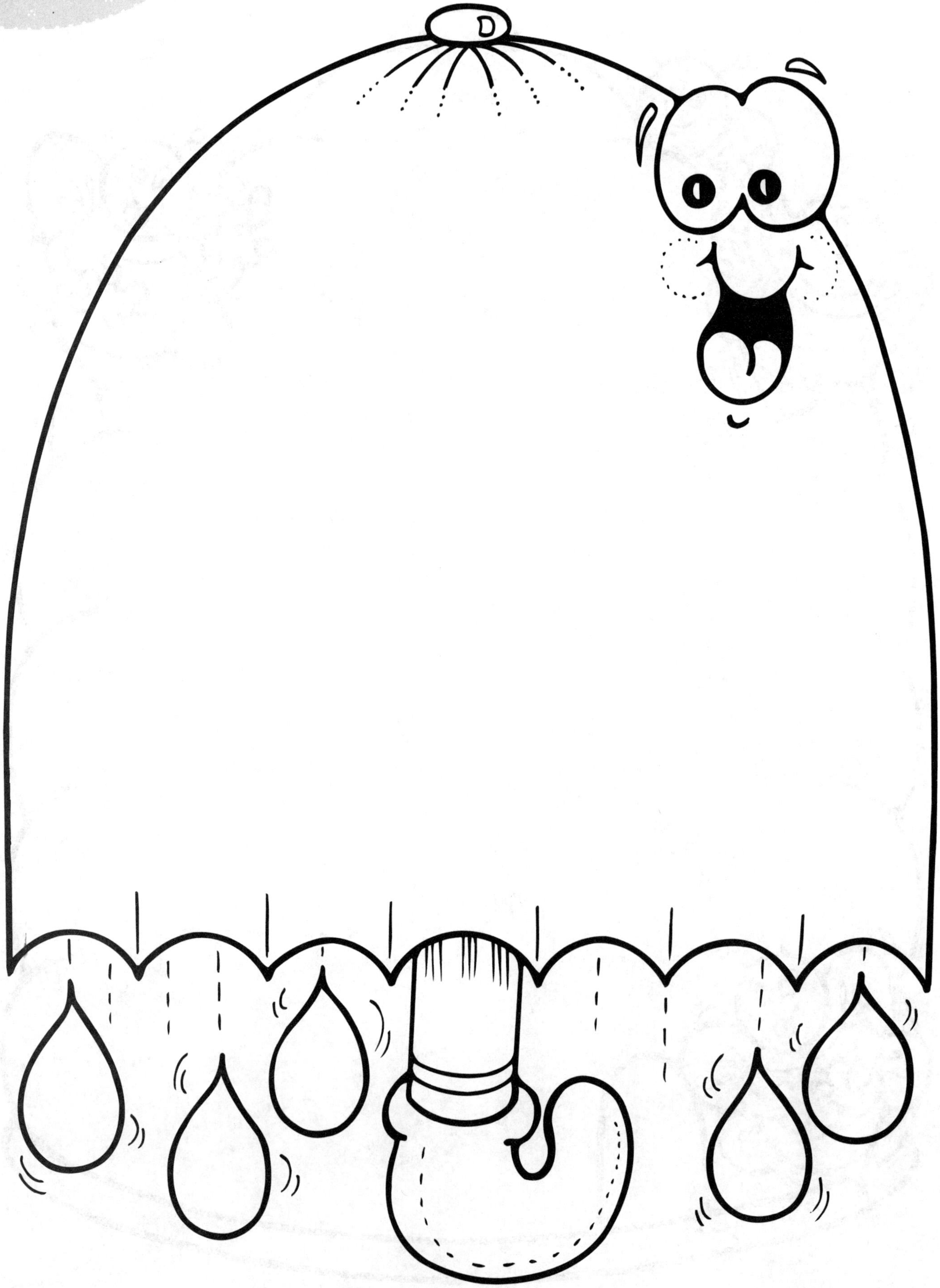
D

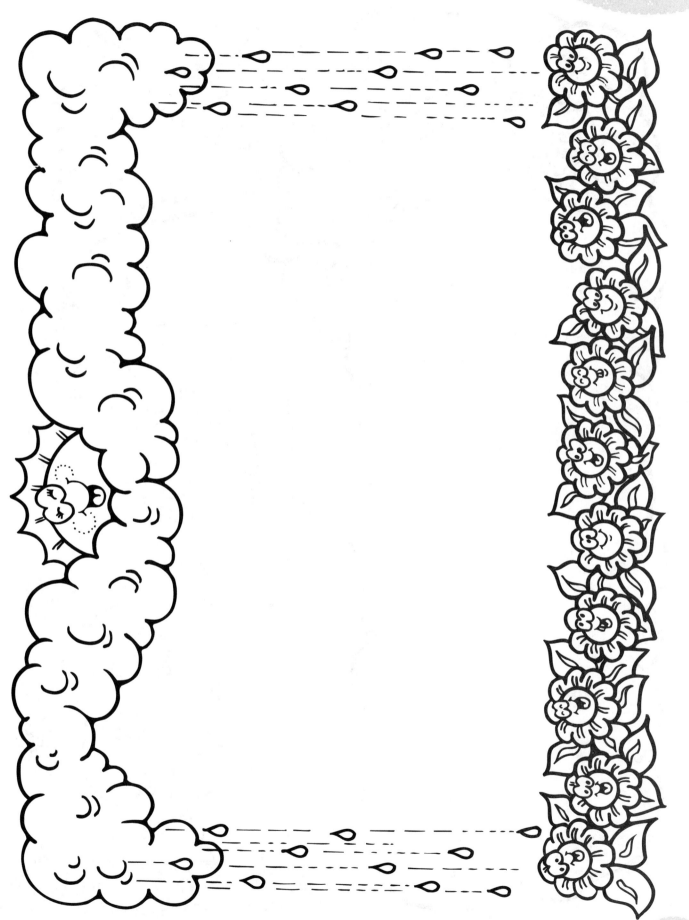

REDUCE

RECYCLE

REUSE

May

Sunday	Monday	Tuesday	Wednesday	Thursday	Friday	Saturday

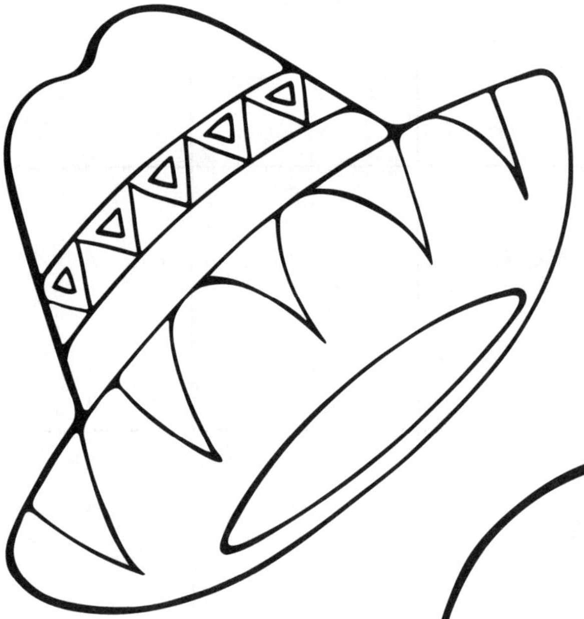

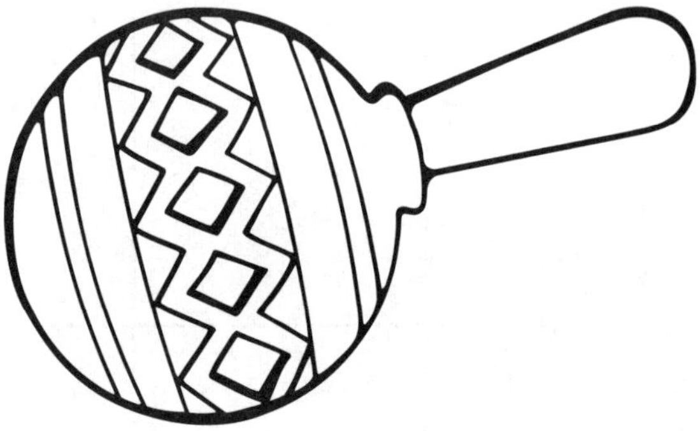

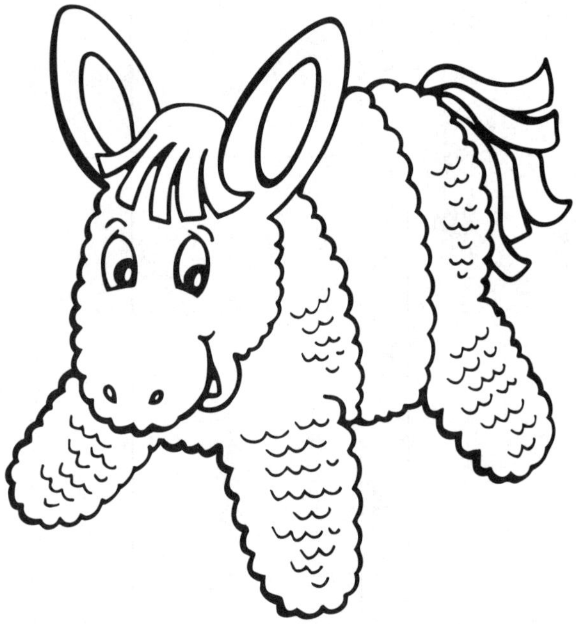

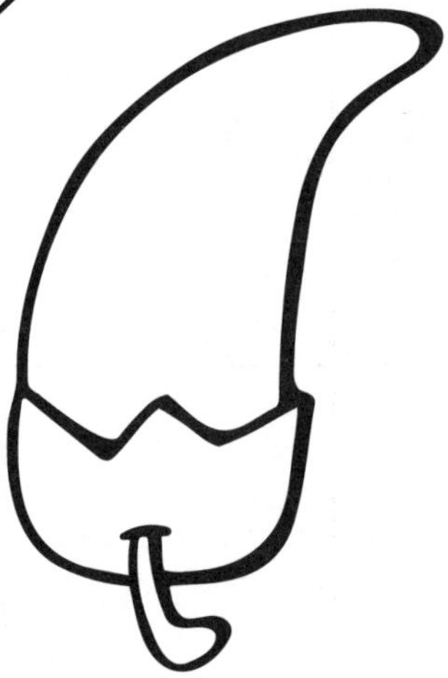

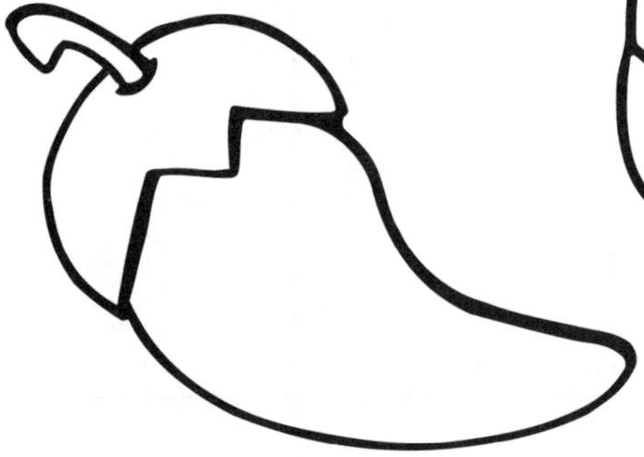

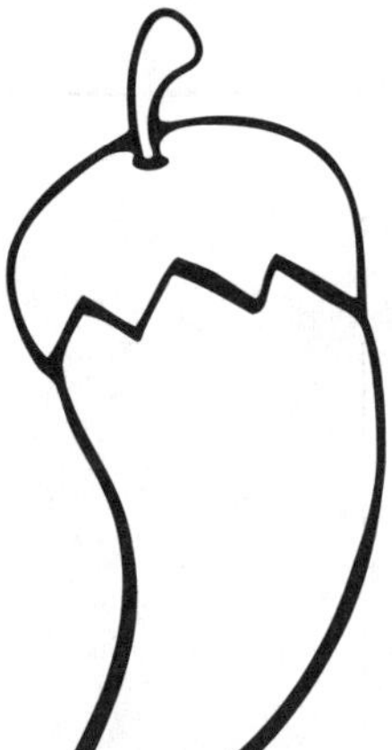

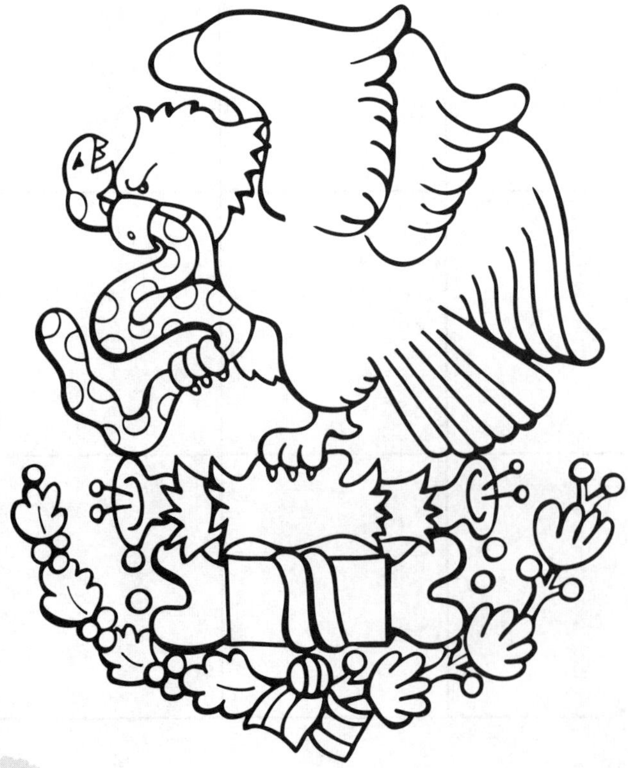

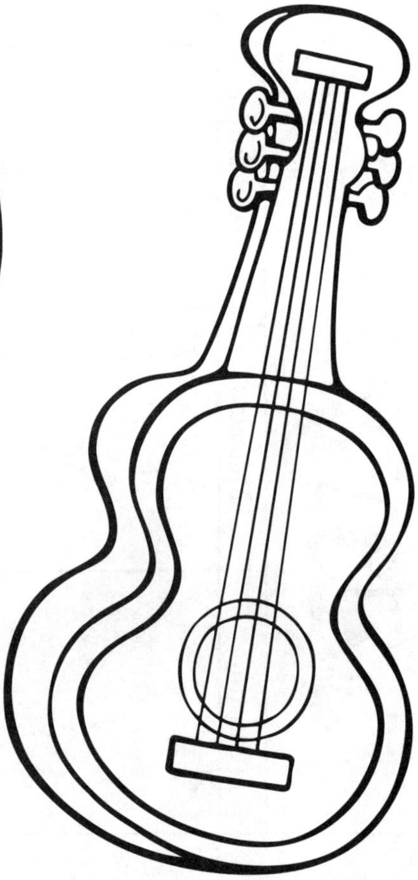

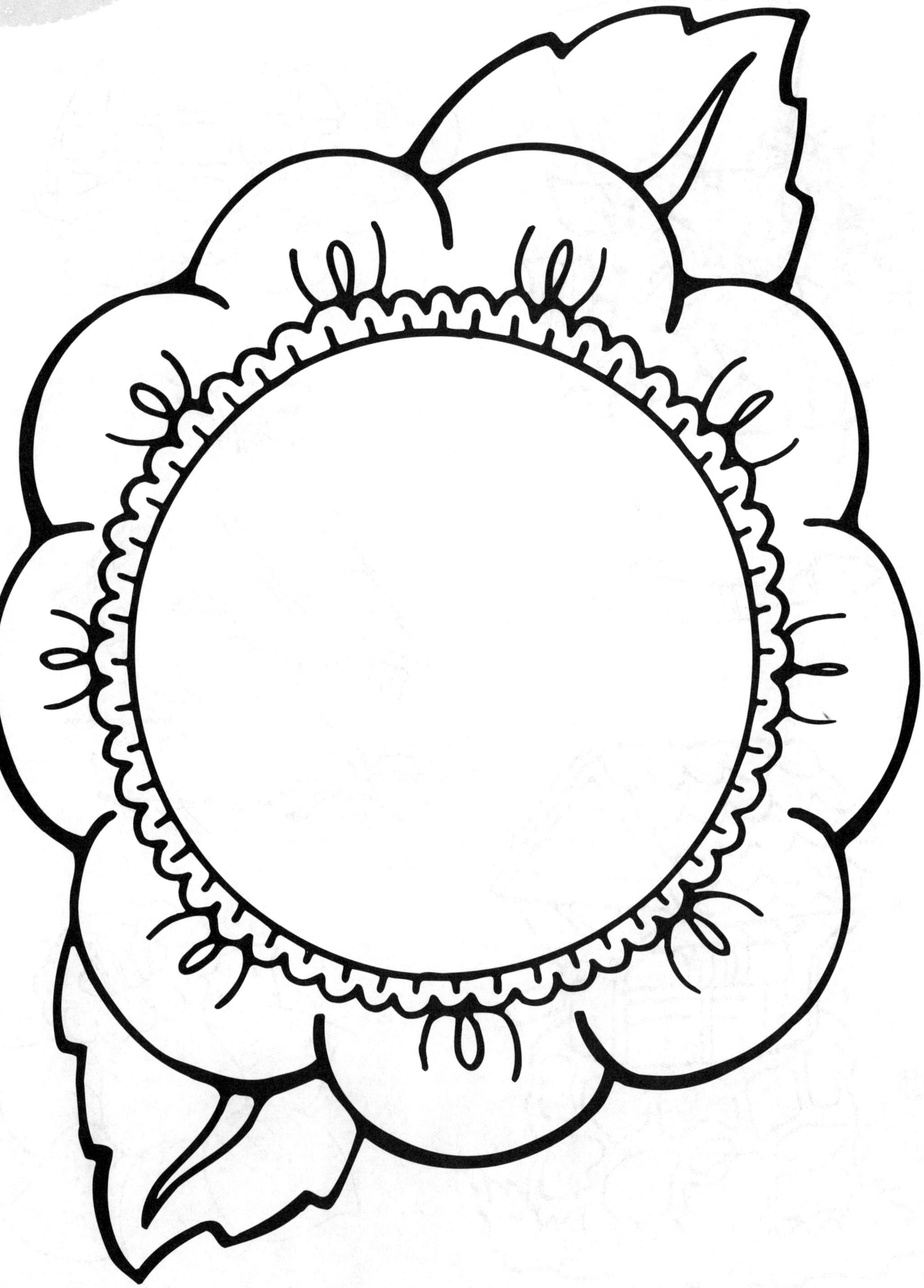

June

Sunday	Monday	Tuesday	Wednesday	Thursday	Friday	Saturday

117

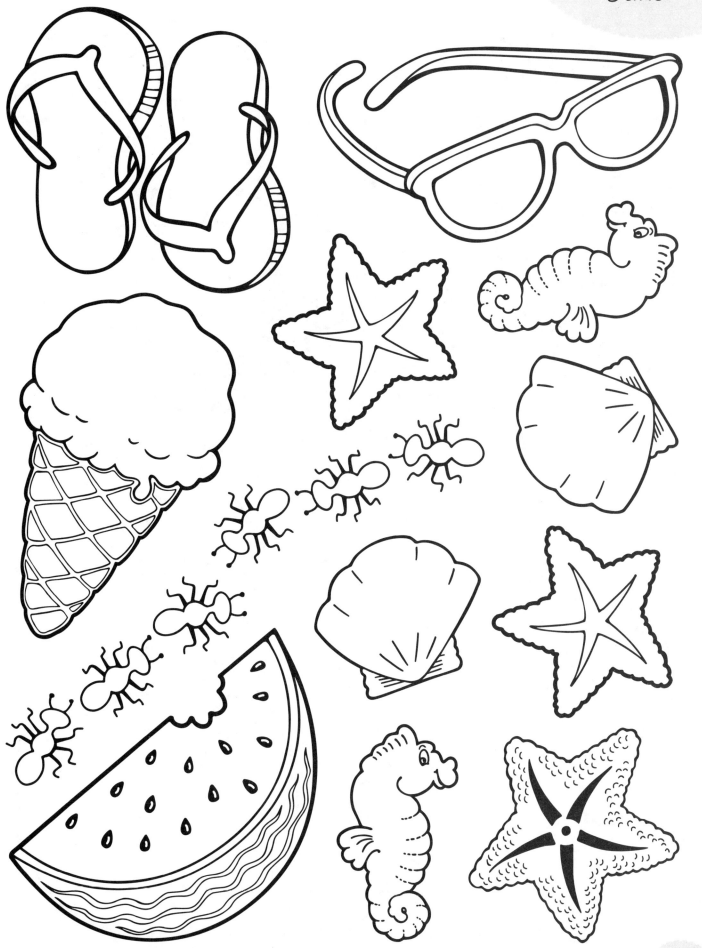

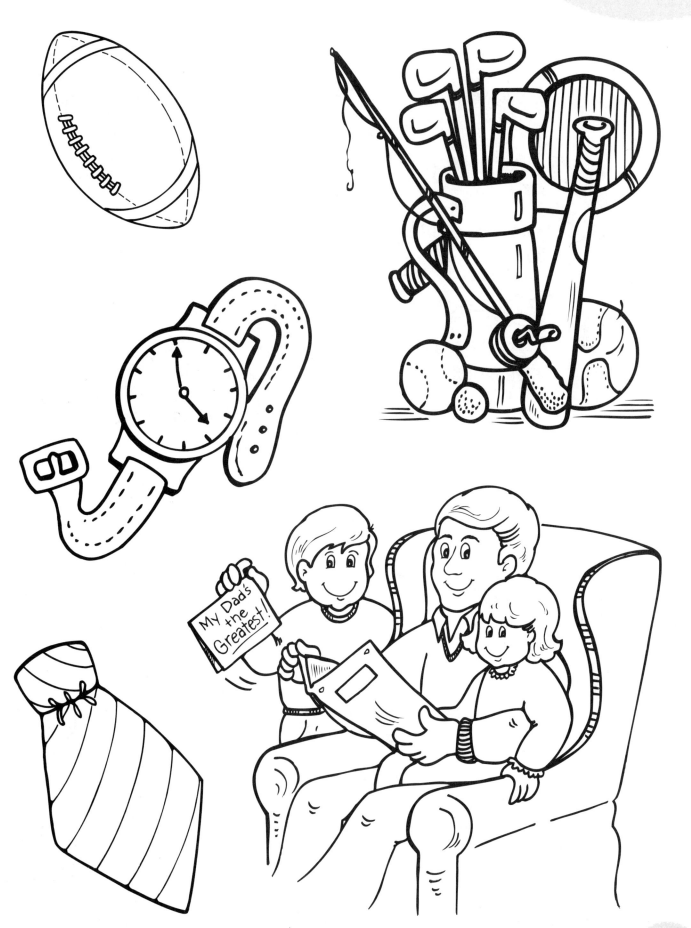

July

Sunday	Monday	Tuesday	Wednesday	Thursday	Friday	Saturday

4th of July!

July

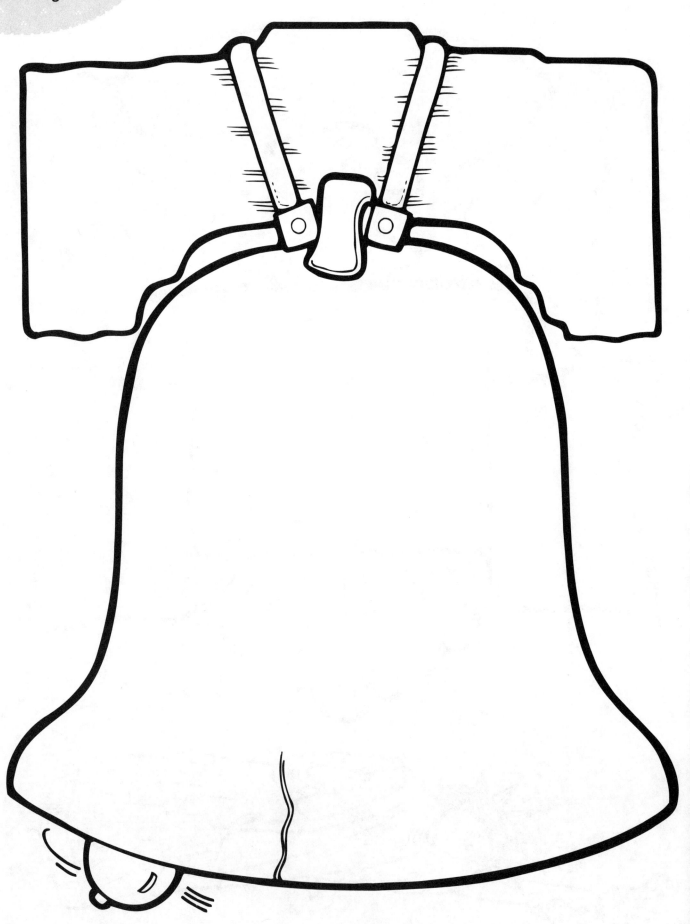

July

July

August

Sunday	Monday	Tuesday	Wednesday	Thursday	Friday	Saturday